The Magic of Space Clearing

Presented by Spirit School by Jodie Harvala

www.JodieHarvala.com

THE MAGIC OF SPACE CLEARING

Presented by Spirit School

By Jodie Harvala

Copyright © 2016. Jodie Harvala.

All Rights Reserved. No part of this publication may be reproduced, distributed, or transmitted in any form or by any means, including photocopying, recording, or other electronic or mechanical methods, without the prior written permission of the publisher, except in the case of brief quotations embodied in critical reviews and certain other noncommercial uses permitted by copyright law.

Published by

Transcendent Publishing
121 104th Avenue
Treasure Island, FL 33706

www.TranscendentPublishing.com

Photographer credit: Melissa Corter

Formatted by Shanda Trofe

ISBN-13: 978-0692638552

ISBN-10: 0692638555

Printed in the United States of America.

Dedicated to my boys ... always.

Contents

Introduction	1
Chapter 1: Spirit Helpers	1
Dream Team Exercise	6
Working on Blocks	9
Clearing Energy	9
Clearing the House	12
Chapter 2: Body Dowsing	17
Body Clearing	17
Witness Protection	17
Body Scan	18
Body Clearing Partner Exercise	23
Chapter 3: the Mirror Effect	27
How our Bodies Mirror our Homes	27
Good Vibrations	37
Chapter 4: Chakras	53
Introduction	53

Root Chakra – 1st Chakra	55
Sacral Plexus – 2nd Chakra	63
Solar Plexus – 3rd Chakra	73
Heart Chakra – 4th Chakra	80
Throat Chakra – 5th Chakra	87
Third Eye – 6th Chakra	94
Crown – 7th Chakra	100
Chapter 5: Clearing a Space	**107**
Clearing a Space Outdoors	107
Front Door	111
Family or Client	114
Basement or Lower Level	117
Main Floor	120
Conclusion	**127**
Bonus Section: Tools	**131**
About the Author	**137**

Introduction

Have I told you how excited I am to launch this book?! I have been waiting years to teach this information and magic to a wide variety of people all over the country and now it's coming true! WOOHOO!

A few thing you may want to know...

This is the very first self-study program from THE SPIRIT SCHOOL and YOU are making HISTORY! Oh if you could see my face right now! All smiles!

How to work through this book:

I have broken the course into modules so you can take one at a time and really dig into it before you move on to the next.

My recommendation on how to work through this course is to read through everything right off the bat because it will give you some sense of what the steps look like and what it is that you're stepping into.

Clearing a space or clearing a body is something that everyone can do, and I am confident that the info that I have included will be a great foundation for you to start on your own clearing journey.

Think of this course as the foundation, and if you feel guided you can take more advanced courses, but even if you decide to stick with this basic info, you will have incredibly powerful experiences. The more you practice, the more information will show up for you! It's just how the natural progression of clearing happens.

Once committed to a clearing course, energy will show up almost immediately to help the energy start to clear. I had a client tell me once that as soon as we booked the appointment she felt she had to go answer the door and when she opened it in her mind's eye, she saw a whole team of angels with cleaning gear like brooms and dust mops and buckets and they all started cleaning her house energetically. What a fun validation of the energy that happens as soon as the commitment starts.

Be patient with yourself and please feel free to ask questions as you walk through this program.

But know before you e-mail, the very first question you will get from me is, "Have you asked your angels and guides for answers?" If you tell me that you have and you don't hear anything I will gently tell you to try again. This course is for you to allow the answers to come to you and through you and the only way to do that is through practice. I love to hear experiences and I love to hear the stories and the clarity that comes after the clearing has been walked through. Please share!

You will also receive the *Meeting Your Guides Meditation* to assist you in finding out who your Spirit Guides are! It's a great meditation and perfect for those getting started on the clearing journey!

Simply follow this link http://bit.ly/meetyourguides to download your copy of the meditation!

I wish you clear energy and spiritual wellness throughout this course!

Now is the time to invite all your angels and helpers in to assist you in the course!

Start to watch for signs and validations that they are with you!

Jodie Harvala

Jodie@JodieHarvala.com

www.JodieHarvala.com

www.TheSpiritSchool.com

1
Spirit Helpers

WHO IS ON YOUR SPIRIT HELPER TEAM?

This week we want to concentrate on both starting to clear but also getting experience with who has your spiritual back.

A few fun ways to experiment with your spirit peeps.

This is a really fun and simple way to start to recognize who is on your helper team. We all have guides and angels and loved ones that are here for our support and assistance. If you have ever felt alone I have to share with you, we are NEVER alone. Spirit is always at our side to offer support and help when we ASK for it.

Because we have free will, spirit does need our permission to step in to assist and help us. Start asking and most of all start to receive!

Learning and creating a relationship with our helpers and team is a huge part of working with intuition and spirit. It's a fun process and if you can really focus on the fun part it's even easier! Play with them—ask for signs and symbol and validation in fun ways.

Spirit is here to help. They are excited we are learning and growing and expanding. A lot of us take this work so seriously it takes some of the magic out of the plan. Loosen up and have a good time with this. We are meant to be in joy and happiness when we do this work. It's less draining and creates some incredible experiences!

I have outlined a few ways to start the process of learning who your spirit helpers are. Take your time. Be gentle. Don't worry if it doesn't come through right off the bat. It takes some time and they will show up when you least expect it!

Dream Team Head Table Exercise

Picture a round table.

You take one seat at that table.

Who would you want to be your right hand man/woman?

For example, mine is my protector—that is just where he presents himself and it works perfectly for me.

To my left is Archangel Gabriel—my Guardian Angel.

To the middle left is Seraphina—she presents as a badass buff chick who steps in when I need strength in life.

To my middle right is Chief—my huge Native American guide who is a Chief and I call him that. He is HUGE and wears red and turquoise in his feathers.

In front of me is God—the way my God shows up.

I also recognize a money guide, a Buddha (my reiki guide), loved ones, of course, and even a business guru that has showed up much more clearly this year.

This has taken me YEARS to be able to recognize the energy of all of these guides as well as get the validation that they are around. Please be patient with this exercise. Let yourself play—even take a moment and just fill in those spaces with who you would hope would be on your Spiritual Dream Team!

The best part of that is they will show up for you!

When you do work on it I want you to get into the basics of working with your spirit and working with that spirit helper team.

A few ideas to get you started:

Do I have a spirit helper team?   Yes or No (EVERYONE has one): _____

Do I have 4 people on my spirit helper team? 5? 6? 7?

Yes or No: _____ How many?: _____

(A little hint: your spiritual dream team is not just your loved ones that have crossed—dream team is guides and angels and ascended masters – the big guys!)

Is my helper team present with me each day? Yes or No: _____

Is my team excited to build this relationship with me? Yes or No: _____

Does my team have a message for me? Yes or No: _____

Will that message come to me in the next week? Yes or No: _____

Will they be teaching me something with that message? Yes or No: _____

A few hints when asking these questions: we all have a dream team! And sometimes our head comes in and gets a little negative and we hear all sorts of lies. Here is what I know for me—we all have guides and angels and they are always at a point of wanting to build a relationship with us and almost always have a message for us, even if it's just a simple *you are loved* message.

They will send validation that they are around and sometimes it takes a little practice to let that in. So please be patient with yourself.

You can ask for names, of course. It's more of a human thing to want to know the name. They are not really connected to that piece. Here is the secret to getting to know what the name is.

Ask.

Yep. Just ask. Listen. Ask for validation.

Call on your team to assist you in all your clearing practices.

Now! Let's get started with the clearing piece!

Working on Blocks

When you find a block one simple way to clear is to use color. It's actually one of my absolute favorite ways to clear energy when it comes up.

Clearing Energy

Body: Find the block

Where is the block in the body?

What shape is it? What color is it?

What emotion is tied to it?

Find the small window of light within the darkness – it could look like a little pinhole of light.

Start to send a rainbow or color that you are guided to send to that energy.

Let it transform that energy from the inside out-

Breathe big deep breaths as you do this exercise. If you are working with a client, then have them do the breathing so that the energy keeps moving.

You will get a sense of completion once the energy has been transformed.

Notes/Thoughts/Reflections

_____

_____

_____

The *Magic* of Space Clearing

ALWAYS fill the energy back up with the rainbow energy so that it does not attract the same junk energy from before. This is a big step that not everyone pays attention to. Please do.

When we transform and empty energy out we always want to fill it back up with something in a higher vibration. It's a beautiful way to move energy and create a safe space inside yourself.

I really do love this type of clearing and find it so powerful! I hope you do too!

Clearing the Home

Find a space that feels blocked within your home-

Where is it?

What shape is it?

What color is it?

What emotion is tied to it?

Do you hold any fear of it? If so, why? And if you need assistance please get a hold of me immediately! DON'T FEED THE FEAR—just examine it and be witness to it.

Find the window of light, start to send the color that your dream team offers to you or that you feel guided to send and watch the transformation.

Tell me how the space felt before and after you cleared the energy.

What do you notice? What do you feel? What do you know? Use all your senses!

Journal the before and after feelings and what you notice:

2
Body Dowsing

Body Clearing

When we talk about Body Clearing we are talking about clearing the energy within and around the body. The world has so many modalities to do this so this is not the only way to clear energy in and around your body; it is just one way. I have found clearing my energy and learning to maintain and protect my energy has been key in creating a healthy state of being. It's been one of the biggest challenges I have had to grow from, to be honest.

Witness Protection

As a sensitive person, and I know you are if you are taking this course, it's important for us to practice Witness Protection. I call it that because we need to learn to witness the world around us and protect or maintain our energy. I prefer maintain our energy but it sure doesn't sound as fun as Witness Protection.

Personally, I call in Archangel Michael to assist me in the process. I invoke his beautiful protective blue-colored energy to come not only around my body, but I have learned to invite that energy IN to my body. If you are challenged with receiving, this will be a great way to practice allowing that magical energy in each day. I do this each morning before my feet hit the floor. Consistency is KEY in this process.

I see energy workers get burnt out ALL the time because they do not learn to maintain energy within themselves. They can pay for it with body pain, aches, burn out, illness, anxiety, fatigue, sleeplessness, extra weight gain and so many more ailments.

So from now on you don't get to brush your teeth until you call in the angels to help you with your Witness Protection! Again, the world has lots of ways to protect such as white light, stones or crystals, prayers, and angels. Experiment with what creates a safe space for you.

Body Scan

When you start to work with your body or even another person's, you will want to do a body scan. This is where those clairs come into practice.

When scanning a body, it can be through feeling the energy around the body and feeling where the energy gets sticky, heavy or dense. Where your hand slows down. Where you feel hot or cold. Sometimes you can feel the vibration slow down or even get prickly and edgy.

You can listen for the energy to create noise or hissing sounds; sometimes the angels will tell you where the blocks are. The guides and angels that assist you will allow the words or sensations into your mind's eye.

Some of you will be able to see the person's aura or even the darker spots inside or on the outside of the body.

These blocks are just energy and typically have emotions surrounding them. So as you feel those dense areas also start to notice and ask what emotion is present. We hold emotion in our bodies and that's not always a healthy thing to do. Dense emotion can be a huge piece of the ailments we have in life. Learning to feel your way through life and creating tools on how to move them out of your body is what this course is all about. Clear your energy and the energy can move and create the freedom we all crave.

Take it slow and pay attention. I have given you several leading questions to get you started, and with practice, you will see the signs and symbols and how spirit works directly with you in the way that works best for your intuition. Most of all, have some fun with this!

We start with the body scan!

What do you feel?

What do you notice?

What temperature do you feel?

What does it smell like?

Do you hear anything?

What emotion do you feel?

Is it thick or thin?

Does it feel like a person or animal?

Do you feel the shape of the energy?

Is it inside the body or attached to the body?

What color is that energy?

Can you speak to it?

What does it want to say?

Why is it here?

Does it give direction on how to release it?

What is the story?

What do your "Spirit Guides" tell you?

What does your gut tell you?

What does your head tell you?

Is the energy ready to leave? Why or why not?

Notes / Thoughts / Reflections

_____
_____
_____
_____
_____
_____

Body Clearing Partner Exercise

Pick a partner to work with or even a friend.

Touch base with your partner—get permission first and then start to use color crayons to make a drawing of the energy in the person's body that you will pick up on before the partner tells you what is going on within their own body.

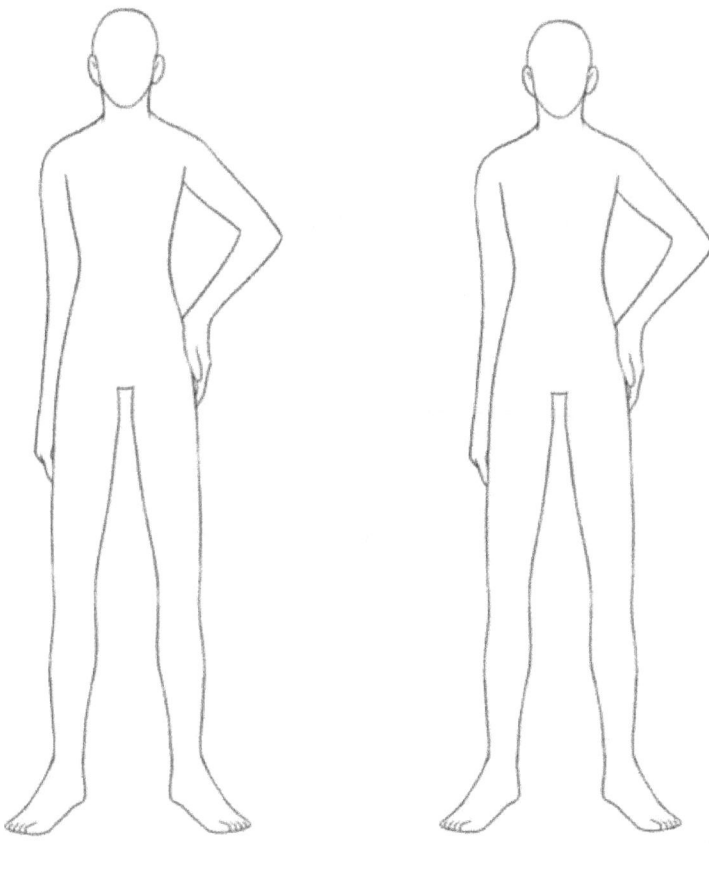

Before-   After-

Work with your "Spirit Guides" on how to clear the energy and then draw the body again AFTER the clearing.

Body Dowsing is multi-layered like all clearing:

4 Levels:
- Body
- Mind
- Emotional
- Spiritual

Things that you may see as symbols:
- Ropes
- Ties
- Grey energy or dark energy
- Smoke
- Fire
- Snakes
- Faces
- Scary Forms

Spirit will use your knowledge to speak to you on how to clear the energy that is coming up to clear. Trust your symbols and start a diary of them throughout this course.

Check into each layer.

Notes / Thoughts / Reflections

3
The Mirror Effect

How our bodies mirror our homes

Think of our homes—we have different levels in most homes. Note: you can still use this scenario even with apartments.

The Basement- The foundation of the home

The Main Floor- The heart of the home

The Upstairs- Our mind

When clearing energy, you will want to notice everything both in front of you and around you. The universe speaks to us in so many ways. I have noticed simple things like a picture on the wall that speaks volumes to energy that needs to be cleared.

A woman wanted her home cleared and wanted to attract a mate.

Over her bed was a picture of a beautiful couple entwined together—a great way to let the universe know what you want. However, she also had a picture on the wall next to her bed, a gorgeous picture of a strong single woman.

Mixed messages to the universe—right! We spoke about all her fears regarding giving up her perceived freedom when in a relationship. It was such a great lesson. Look all around you for the signs!

Anytime I am clearing for a person we start in the basement, I ask what is happening with the person and anyone that lives in the house. This will always give you a clue on what is happening both in the home and if anything is showing up in someone's body.

Exercise

Go either to your basement or just look at the floor if you are in a condo or apartment.

What do you notice?

Do you have any cracks?

What does that mean for you?

Are things a mess?

Record your findings—including anything you feel, sense, or know!

Think of your eyes:

What do you see?

Look out the windows of the home—what do you see?

Notes / Thoughts / Reflections

___

What do you hear?

Ask what is on the radio or TV?

Do they argue a lot? Do you hear a lot of chaos or static?

Notes / Thoughts / Reflections

___
___
___
___
___
___
___
___
___
___
___
___
___
___
___
___
___
___
___
___
___
___
___
___

Think of your mouth:

The front door—what comes in and what goes out?

Is it love or is it fear?

Notes / Thoughts / Reflections

These can all be very important clues to the energy that needs to be cleared in each home.

Good Vibrations!

For each **emotion** there is a **vibration.**

This is something you can work on forever! But to get you started I want to talk about common emotions that show up when clearing homes.

When we talk about clearing, most times it's all about the emotions that are stuck or blocked. This affects the home and the people within the home and prevents them from moving forward. This happens in our bodies as well. Over time you will learn to recognize that each emotion is tied to a vibration. Those vibrations are showing us the rate and density of that emotion. So think about happiness, that is a high vibration and feels light and airy and fun. Now think about anger. It's lower, harder, slower, denser. This week's module is smaller but it is one of the most important.

This is a way to exercise and use your intuition and skills with your body, mind and spirit and recognize the vibration of each emotion that comes up for you.

It's very interesting, as I do clearing I find that certain houses will show up when I am clearing certain things in my own life. As you heal, I heal. As I heal, you heal. It's a group effort and energy attracts energy. As we clear layer after layer the powerful piece of supporting someone in walking through a tough journey that you have walked yourself is one of the most powerful experiences in the world.

Take your time with this module. Not only is it important to recognize the energy but to also allow that energy to MOVE through you as you release it. It's not our job to hold that energy, it's our job to allow it to move through us. We are not responsible for someone else's energy or emotions.

What I want you to do is tune into each emotions and how it shows up for you. Is it a slow vibration or fast? Wet or dry? High or low? Can you smell it or see it? Where in your body do you feel it? Record what you feel:

Anger:

_____
_____
_____
_____
_____
_____
_____

Happiness:

_____
_____
_____
_____
_____
_____
_____

Sadness:

_____
_____
_____
_____

Grief:

_____
_____
_____
_____
_____
_____
_____

Addiction:

_____
_____
_____
_____
_____
_____
_____

Depression:

_____
_____
_____
_____
_____

Joy:
_____
_____
_____
_____
_____
_____

Money:
_____
_____
_____
_____
_____
_____

Opportunity:
_____
_____
_____
_____
_____

Dreams:

Abuse:

Cancer:

Love:

_____
_____
_____
_____
_____
_____

Pregnancies or Babies:

_____
_____
_____
_____
_____
_____

Death:

_____
_____
_____
_____
_____

Happiness:

_____
_____
_____
_____
_____
_____

Suicide:

_____
_____
_____
_____
_____
_____

Pets:

_____
_____
_____
_____
_____

Illness:
_____
_____
_____
_____
_____
_____
_____

Grandparents:
_____
_____
_____
_____
_____
_____
_____

Nurturing:
_____
_____
_____
_____
_____

Mental Illness:

_____
_____
_____
_____
_____
_____
_____

Bankruptcy:

_____
_____
_____
_____
_____
_____
_____

Support:

_____
_____
_____
_____
_____

Disappointments:

_____
_____
_____
_____
_____
_____

Fear:

_____
_____
_____
_____
_____
_____

Spirit (God of Your Belief):

_____
_____
_____
_____

Angels:

_____
_____
_____
_____
_____
_____
_____

Deceased Loved Ones:

_____
_____
_____
_____
_____
_____
_____

Friends:

_____
_____
_____
_____

Spouse:

_____
_____
_____
_____
_____
_____

Children:

_____
_____
_____
_____
_____
_____

Please feel free to add any additional hits you get throughout this exercise. I have supplied extra space below to record:

_____
_____
_____
_____

4
Chakras

Introduction

The Chakra system is within our bodies and the chakras themselves are energy areas that start at the base of our spine and work all the way through our heads. Now we have many systems like this in our bodies and in our energy fields but this is the basic system and a great place to start!

With this module I wanted to give you a really great but simple run down of the chakras and ideas to clear them as you start your spiritual journey or even if you are very advanced. Our chakra system can affect so many parts and pieces of our energetic make up and learning the basics can give you a starting place when working with clients and any ailments that show up.

I have found that clearing my chakras on a regular basis has been incredibly important in helping with anxiety I used to have. The clearer I keep them, and the better I take care of myself, the clearer the energy that comes through spirit.

If you suffer with anxiety, I highly recommend to start learning and working and clearing the chakra system and see how things improve! I have provided several pages of info and I recommend that you work through each one thoroughly before going forward with the next. Take your time and allow yourself the time to move through them systematically. Your spirit will tell you when it's time to move on.

CHAKRA LOCATION CHART

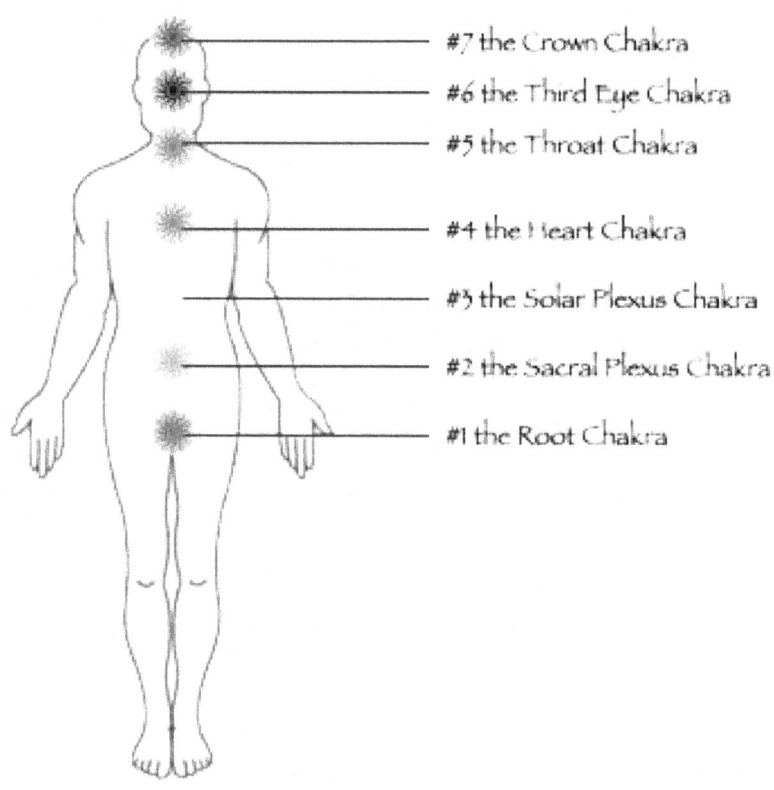

- #7 the Crown Chakra
- #6 the Third Eye Chakra
- #5 the Throat Chakra
- #4 the Heart Chakra
- #3 the Solar Plexus Chakra
- #2 the Sacral Plexus Chakra
- #1 the Root Chakra

Root Chakra – 1st Chakra

Location: Base of spine

Color: Red

Emotion: Stability and security

Gland: Endocrine - adrenals

Organs and Body Parts: Large intestine, rectum, hips and thighs

When Balanced: Centered, survival, security, personal safety, grounded

Out of Balance: Self Indulgence, self-centered, insecurity, grief, depression

Health Effects: Hemorrhoids, constipation, sciatica

10 ways to activate as well as get in touch with your Root Chakra

1. See red, wear red, draw with red, breathe with red—encompass the color red.

2. Dance. Move the hips and wiggle that behind!

3. Get on your yoga mat. Breathe in all the way down to the base of your spine.

4. Take a shower.

5. Zen out on a walk.

6. Get a pedicure.

7. Imagine roots coming from the top of your head all the way down through your spine and into the earth. You can also imagine those roots going through your feet.

8. Barefoot in the earth—wiggle the toes and dig into the dirt! I have lots of friends who keep dirt in the house even in the winter for when they need extra grounding.

9. Engage in the present time—Root Chakra helps to keep us grounded and PRESENT.

10. Connect with Mother Earth!

Glands: Endocrine – Adrenals

Organs and Body Parts: Large Intestine, Rectum, Hips and Thighs

When our Root Chakra is out of balance it can also affect our endocrine system.

Think of our fight or flight. Do you get worked up easily? Living in fear? Worry is a main emotion that you work with each day.

This energy starts to tax our systems, wears our bodies down, can effect thyroid function as well. There is lots of info online to different body parts if you wish to research.

I suggest acupuncture, supplements, walks, meditation, journaling and burning, a good cry, good night sleep, talk therapy, reiki- and many other ways to help ease our busy bodies.

If you are having issues with parts of your body such as large intestine, digestion, rectum, hemorrhoids, hips and thighs, pay attention to your Root Chakra for healing benefits and to get your body back in balance.

Exercise

I encourage you to close your eyes— bring your attention to the base of your spine, the red glowing ball of energy that is your Root Chakra. From that Root Chakra you will imagine that beautiful red light streaming into the earth and connecting with the heart of the earth. Mother Earth is here to help us feel nurtured and safe.

Mother Earth is here to offer a place to connect to for those who don't feel safe or need extra comfort in times of stress. Through your Root Chakra she will fill your body with energy that fills up not only your Root Chakra but your entire body with a glowing red and or pink light of earth love.

Those that deal with any type of anxiety: work on connecting with Mother Earth each and every day to connect you to that safe and grounding energy. Simply close your eyes and imagine Mother Earth surrounding you with her beautiful energy.

Stability and Security

These are the key emotions around the Root Chakra.

Take a moment. Are you feeling safe and secure in this very moment?

Have you ever taken that time to feel what that feels like in your body?

What key elements in your life would create a space of safety and security?

Maybe you have never felt safe—old wounds from childhood or when you were a teenager.

Maybe even events in adulthood that are effecting you even today!

First off, I am not a doctor nor a licensed counselor, so please seek medical and licensed help if needed when digging into old wounds.

When events in life happen, they can leave residual energy within the chakras in our bodies

This week we are working on healing old wounds that may have upset the balance of our Root Chakra.

Wounds that have upset our safety and security, and now spirit says its time. It's time to heal those wounds so you can stand tall and show up as the amazing person that you are!

BREATHE

IDEAS to Connect to Root Chakra

BREATHE: Each day, stop at least five times in a day and breathe into your Root Chakra.

DANCE: Turn the music up once a day each day this week and dance for at least five minutes paying attention to the hips and lower back and booty ☺ Shake it!

WRITE: Close those eyes. Picture your root chakra.

Breathe into it and let your Root Chakra talk to you.

What wounds are still there from childhood or adulthood that can be let go and forgiven or transmuted?

LOOK: Use your imagination and find those denser energies within the chakra and ask why they are there. What are they needing to move through you and let go?

DO: What can you do to feel more balanced in your Root Chakra. Listen to and create a plan for this week on balancing your Root Chakra.

NEW People: I know this may be new to you and seem a little weird or strange in what we are asking you to do. JUST DO IT ☺ This work can be strange and weird and all sorts of adventures can come from it but more importantly all sorts of healing can come from just trying some of the exercises.

Some will work for you and some wont—that is OK.

If you don't "SEE" your Root Chakra, use your imagination. Make it up. You will feel your energy shift into a different vibration when you start to get the information your body wants you to hear.

Feel free to post your results and questions in the group.

Notes / Thoughts / Reflections

The Sacral Plexus Charka – 2nd Chakra

Location: It's between pubic bone and the belly button

Color: Orange

Emotion and Energy: Creativity and sexuality, happiness, confidence, resourcefulness

Associated gland: Ovaries

Organs and body parts: Reproductive system , bladder and kidney

When Balanced: Patience, endurance, self-confidence, and well-being

Out of Balance: Frustration, anxiety, fear, frigidness, and over-sexed

Health Effects: Fertility problems, menstruation problems, menopause difficulties, and kidney or bladder problems

Orange is the color of success and relates to self-respect—having the ability to give ourselves the freedom to be ourselves and helps expand our interests and activities. Brings joy to our workday and strengthens our appetite for life! Orange is the best emotional stimulant. It connects us to our senses and helps to remove inhibitions and makes us independent and social.

10 ways to get in touch with your Sacral Plexus Chakra:

1. I feel… _____

2. I feel creative when I... _____

3. I feel confident when... _____

4. I feel sexual when... _____

5. I feel resourceful when... _____

6. I feel frustrated when... _____

7. I feel anxiety when... _____

8. I feel fear when... _____

9. Put your hands on your belly. What does it have to say?

_____

10. Write a letter from your Second Chakra to yourself. What does it say? What does it need? How much is it effecting how you FEEL each day?

_____
_____
_____
_____
_____
_____
_____
_____
_____
_____
_____
_____

The *Magic* of Space Clearing

Exercise

Close your eyes.

Take a breath, connect to the earth, create a bond between the Root Chakra and Mother Earth. Breathe in!

Move your energy up to the second energy center—the Sacral Chakra, a bright orange ball of light that sits above the Root Chakra.

Breathe in the earth energy to that space. Bring in bright orange light to clear any dense energy, any blocks, any energy that may be stuck and wanting to move, and allow freedom into the creative center of your body.

Ask your soul, your spirit, what type of creative outlet would add joy and FUN to your life right now. Something new? Something you did as a child? Something that will make you laugh. Something that will fill you up with joy.

Have you forgotten what that might be? Maybe what used to bring you joy doesn't seem to work any longer. It's a time for renewal. A time for allowing new blessings into your body and your life.

Breathe in that orange energy and allow it to fill you up!

Self-confidence, Creativity, Resourcefulness

The Sacral Plexus Chakra is all about self-confidence, creativity, and resourcefulness.

Self-confidence. This is a big can of worms for people sometimes, isn't it? This week I want you to work on that piece of you that sometimes doesn't feel as confident.

AND I want you to work on that part of you that IS totally confident.

How can you wrap those two together and create an agreement between the two of them? How can they work together?

What does the part of you that doesn't feel confident need? What does the super confident part need to stick around and keep going? How can they become a team? Sometimes those parts of us just need a voice. They just need a place to create expression.

What is the expression all about? What is it that your soul really wants to express right now?

BREATHE

IDEAS to connect to Root Chakra

Each day, stop at least five times in a day and breathe into your 2nd Chakra.

WRITE: Close those eyes. Picture your 2nd Chakra.

Breathe into it and let your 2nd Chakra talk to you.

What wounds are still there from childhood or adulthood that can be let go and forgiven or transmuted?

CREATE: What can you create and express this week that feel creative and FUN.

LOOK: Use your imagination and find those denser energies within the chakra and ask why they are there. What are they needing to move through you and let go?

DO: What can you do to feel more balanced in your 2nd Chakra. Listen to and create a plan for this week on balancing your 2nd Chakra.

Some will work for you and some wont—that is OK.

If you don't "SEE" your 2nd Chakra, use your imagination. Make it up. You will feel your energy shift into a different vibration when you start to get the information your body wants you to hear.

I love and accept myself. I freely express my creativity. I enjoy a passionate life.

Notes / Thoughts / Reflections

_____
_____
_____
_____
_____
_____
_____
_____
_____
_____

The Solar Plexus – 3rd Chakra

Color: Yellow

Location: It's between base of sternum and navel

Emotion and Energy: Personal Power and self esteem

Associated gland: Adrenals

Organs and body parts: Liver, pancreas, gall bladder, small intestine and stomach

Balanced: Personal power, self-motivation, decisions, willfulness, and self-image

Out of Balance: Powerlessness, greed, low self-esteem, doubt, anger, built aggression

Health Effects: Diabetes, ulcers, poor digestion, jaundice, hepatitis, hypoglycemia, gall stones

Yellow is a creative color and relates to self-worth. How we feel about ourselves and how we feel others perceive us. This is the area of the personality, the ego and the intellect. It gives us clarity of thought, increases awareness, and stimulates interest and curiosity. Yellow energy is related to the ability to perceive and understand. The yellow energy connects us to our mental self.

10 ways to get in touch with your 3rd Chakra:

1. I do… _____

2. I do feel _____ about myself

3. I do feel _____ about how others feel about me

4. I do perceive life as _____

5. I do think about _____ most of the time

6. I do_____to myself enough

7. I do not_____to myself enough

8. I do feel my brain wants_____

9. I do feel my heart wants_____

10. I do believe the heart and head want to create_____
_____

Exercise

Close your eyes.

Take a breath. Connect to the earth—create a bond between the Root Chakra and mother earth.

Breathe in! Move your energy up to the second energy center, the Second Chakra, a bright orange ball of light that sits above the Root Chakra. Breathe in the earth energy to that space. Bring in bright orange light to clear any dense energy any blocks, any energy that may be stuck and wanting to move, and allow freedom into the creative center of your body.

Bring in another breath into your 3rd Chakra. Breathe into that yellow light through the 3rd Chakra.

Bring that energy down to Mother Earth and back up through the Root Chakra the 2nd Chakra and back into your 3rd Chakra.

Ask your soul, what is it that brings you to your personal power? How does it feel to be in touch with that personal power?

Have you forgotten what that might be? Maybe what used to bring you a sense of self that doesn't seem to work any longer? It's a time for renewal. A time for allowing new blessings into your body and your life.

Breathe in that yellow energy and allow yourself to find your inner power. This chakra is all about **Personal Power, Self-Esteem, Self-worth.**

Deserving and self-worth are huge subjects these days.

When we are not open to receive or in a space of being closed it's hard to see our value and worth.

This week, notice places that you feel worth—notice when you don't.

We create beliefs and stories around these feelings that may be holding us back from our inner power.

Inner power is following the path for YOU. We like to be included and be part of something but sometimes spirit has a path that is meant just for you. Take a look this week at what you notice about your own path.

Purpose is brought to you each and every day. We just need to recognize it.

BREATHE

Ideas to connect with your Sacral Plexus Chakra

Each day, stop at least five times in a day and breathe into your 3rd Chakra.

WRITE: Close those eyes, picture your 3rd Chakra.

Breathe into it and, let your 3nd chakra talk to you.

What wounds are still there from childhood or adulthood that can be let go and forgiven or transmuted.

CREATE: Draw a picture of what your personal power feels like and post on the page.

LOOK: Use your imagination and find those denser energies within the chakra and ask why they are there- what are they needing to move through you and let go.

DO: What can you do to feel more balanced in your 3nd Chakra.

ASK - Ask for three power words that your 3rd chakra wants you to use.

If you don't "SEE" your 3rd Chakra, use your imagination—make it up. You will feel your energy shift into a different vibration when you start to get the information your body wants you to hear.

> *I am a powerful creator of my life.*
>
> *I easily manifest my desires.*

Notes / Thoughts / Reflections

The *Magic* of Space Clearing

The Heart Chakra – 4th Chakra

Location: Center of heart

Color: Green

Emotion: Love and Nurture

Gland: Endocrine, thymus

Organs and Body Parts: Heart, lungs and breasts

When Balanced: Compassion, acceptance, love, fulfillment, and forgiveness

Out of Balance: Loneliness, insensitivity, emotionally closed, passively, sadness, and overly selfless

Health Effects: Benign breast disease, lung disease, immune related diseases, high blood pressure, heart disease and arthritis

10 ways to activate as well as get in touch with your Heart Chakra

1. Breathe green in and breathe out any blocks. Breathe in green, fill up that heart!

2. Hand on your heart—I am in my heart. Say this aloud several times a day.

3. Open your arms wide. I am open to receive all the great in the universe!!!!! WIDE open arms!

4. Cry. A great way to get in touch with feelings that you may be hiding from.

5. Give someone a hug that lasts more than 30 seconds.

6. Write yourself a love letter.

7. Imagine your Heart Chakra—beautiful green and imagine that green growing and flowing through your body.

8. Music. Anything that makes your heart sing, or your mouth sing! ☺ Music is a heart's best friend.

9. Engage in the present time. Heart space is present at all times.

10. Connect with the four elements: Wind, Water, Earth and Air.

Exercise

I encourage you to close your eyes. Imagine your Root Chakra into the earth—grounding you—bringing that grounding energy up into your 2nd and 3rd Chakra- and up into your Heart Chakra. As your Heart Chakra opens, imagine a beautiful light of green enveloping your heart and your body. As that green energy explodes, reach up into the moon energy. Whenever there is a full moon we can use this energy to help release all that doesn't serve us any longer and refill all that does serve us in the most beautiful light. From spirit, through spirit, and to spirit. Connecting into our heart space can bring you into a space of healing and love. Breathe in green, breathe out blocks. Breathe in green, breathe out blocks.

Love and Nurture

These are the key emotions around the Heart Chakra:

Take a moment. Are you feeling loved and nurtured?

Have you ever taken the time to feel what that feels like in your body?

What key elements in your life would create a space of love and nurturing?

Maybe as an adult the space of feeling loved and nurtured has changed since being a child.

Maybe it's a time to reflect on what creates that feeling of being loved and nurtured as an adult.

Learning self-soothing tools to feel loved and nurtured inside your own heart can take not only some time but some space of being vulnerable. Did you get enough as a child? It could be time to write a few letters to let those emotions flow and then burn them to release them.

Is it hard to let people love you? Take some time explore that. Do you love yourself?

Loving ourselves, is in my opinion, one of the first steps in the healing process. We can move through anything if we can find a space of love inside ourselves.

BREATHE

IDEAS to connect to Heart Chakra

BREATHE: Each day, stop at least five times in a day and BREATHE into your Heart Chakra.

Heart Chakra is about Love.

So this week it's all about loving yourself.

Be patient with yourself though this exercise.

Create a list of thing you LOVE about yourself-

If this is difficult that's OK—just take your time.

Sometimes you may need to write a list of what you don't love about yourself and that will give you a place to start-

I call this shadow work- and looking at our shadows of the heart can be such a healing space.

Each day, create a list of five things you discovered you love about yourself.

POST THEM in our group!

LOVE YOURSELF!

> *I completely love and accept myself! I give and receive love effortlessly!*

Notes / Thoughts / Reflections

Throat Chakra – 5th Chakra

Location: Throat

Color: Blue

Emotion: Communication and self-expression

Gland: Thyroid

Organs and Body Parts: Throat, trachea and vocal cords

When Balanced: Communication, self-expression, creativity, speaking your feelings and inspiration

Out of Balance: Stagnation, obsession, lack of expression or communication

Health Effects: Sore throat, laryngitis, stutter and thyroid problems

10 ways to activate as well as get in touch with your Throat Chakra

1. BLUE: blue scarf, blue necklace, blue stones. Breathe in blue.

2. SING: Sing your heart out. Happy songs, sad songs, angry songs, inspiration songs.

3. Hand on your throat—what does it need to say?

4. Write it out …

5. Humming: Just to get the energy moving. Humming can start to move any stuck energy.

6. Pamper your throat: Honey, warm tea, smile, breathe in steamy moist air. Pay attention to your throat.

7. Imagine roots coming from the top of your head all the way down through your spine and into the earth. You can also imagine those roots going through your feet and bring that energy up to your throat and back down to earth.

8. Be present in communications. Really stick with a communication between you and someone. Look them in the eyes, be interested in what they have to say, speak your truth.

9. Speak from the "I am feeling" space instead of "you make me feel." I am feeling" can change an entire conversation.

10. Connect with your truth. What is it? What are you wanting to say out loud to the world? How can you start that conversation?

Exercise

I encourage you to close your eyes. Bring your attention to the base of your throat to the blue sphere of color is your throat chakra. Notice if it's closed or stuck or maybe even is holding onto some dense energy. Ask if it's ready to clear. Imagine polishing it up and removing any dense or dark energy to encourage this chakra to start moving in a beautiful smooth way.

Mother Earth is here to offer those who don't feel safe or need extra comfort in time of stress a place to connect to and through your Throat Chakra. She will fill your body with energy that fills up not only your Throat Chakra but your entire body with a glowing blue light of speaking from love.

Speaking our truth is a beautiful place to be. Speaking your truth from love is an even better place to be. "What would love say" is a great affirmation when you're working on difficult ways to get your truth to the world. Everything can be said with love. This week start asking what would love say before you start to speak and see what happens with your throat.

Sunny Dawn Johnston has a beautiful movement of "What would love say?" Check out her site for more info.

Communication and Self-Expression

These are the key emotions around the Throat Chakra.

Take a moment. Are you communicating and expressing yourself in positive ways?

Have you ever taken that time to feel what that feels like in your body?

What key elements in your life would create a space of self-expression and communication?

Self-expression, in my opinion, is one of the most important of tools to learn.

Expressing ourselves is a divine right—we are here to express ourselves, our wants, needs and desires.

We all have emotions that we think are bad or sad or resentful or even hateful. Those need to be expressed in a healthy way to keep energy moving in our bodies.

Journal and burning are very healthy ways to get that energy out. Write a letter to the person who you are holding that energy for and release it, then burn it to offer it back to the universe to get back to the light.

Jumping up and down is also a fun way to express the energy as you jump and keep jumping until it gets out and you start laughing instead – this is a great one for kids.

All those emotions are normal human expressions and must be honored in the way that we express those emotions.

BREATHE

IDEAS to connect to Throat Chakra

BREATHE: Each day- stop at least five times in a day and breathe into your Throat Chakra.

SING: Turn the music up once a day each day this week and sing for at least five minutes paying attention to the throat! Sing loud people!

WRITE: Close those eyes. Picture your Throat Chakra.

Breathe into it and let your Throat Chakra talk to you.

What wounds are still there from childhood or adulthood that can be let go and forgiven or transmuted?

LOOK: Use your imagination and find those denser energies within the chakra and ask why they are there. What are they needing to move through you and let go?

DO: What can you do to feel more balanced in your Throat Chakra? Listen to and create a plan for this week on balancing your Throat Chakra.

NEW People: I know this may be new to you and seem a little weird or strange in what we are asking you to do—JUST

DO IT ☺ This work can be strange and weird and all sorts of adventures can come from it but more importantly all sorts of healing can come from just trying some of the exercises.

> *I always express myself truthfully and clearly. My thoughts are positive.*

Some will work for you and some wont—that is OK.

If you don't "SEE" your Throat Chakra, use your imagination. Make it up—you will feel your energy shift into a different vibration when you start to get the information your body wants you to hear.

Feel free to post your results and questions in the group.

Notes / Thoughts / Reflections

_____
_____
_____
_____
_____
_____
_____

Third Eye Charka – 6ᵗʰ Chakra

Third Eye Chakra is the 6th Chakra and is responsible for what we refer to as "the sixth sense". The Chakra connects us to our internal intuitions and is responsible for the sharp senses, the ability to read the future and receive non-verbal messages. Through the Third Eye we communicate with the world and can even receive messages from the past and from the future. It grants us our sense of observation.

Location of the Chakra in the Body: The center of the forehead, between the eyes.

Color: Indigo

Emotion: Intuition, inspiration and insight

Gland: Pituitary

Organs and Body Parts: Eyes, ears and sinuses

When Balanced: Intellectual and psychic abilities/inner vision, visualization and imagination projection and perception

Out of Balance: Difficulty focusing in life, detachment, intellectual stagnation and fuzzy thinking

Health Effects: Eye diseases, hearing loss, schizophrenia and headaches

Balance your Third Eye Chakra: Ways to increase Indigo Energy:

1. Practice Meditation to develop your intuition.

2. Use aroma therapeutic essential oils such as Patchouli, Myrrh and Olibanum or oils you are guided to.

3. Add purple and indigo colors to your wardrobe, even a scarf can assist the flow of energy.

4. Choosing music that is classical in nature such as Mozart, Beethoven, and Bach can enhance the energies flowing to the Third Eye Chakra. But I would also say any music that floats your boat will work!! Music is an amazing healer.

5. Gemstones associated with the Third Eye Chakra are amethyst, tourmaline and tanzanite.

6. Quiet time or meditation to connect with yourself and rest.

7. Focused meditation such as lighting a candle and staring into it for a several minutes to allow your mind to shut down?

8. Coloring! Did you know it's an active meditation? Anything creative is always good for the intuition and the Third Eye Chakra.

BREATHE

IDEAS to connect to Third Eye Chakra

BREATHE: Each day- stop at least five times in a day and breathe into your Third Eye Chakra.

ANGELS: Connecting with your angels is a fantastic way to get in touch with your intuition and Third Eye.

EYES: Close those eyes. Imagine a beautiful single eye right between your eyebrows, Is it open? It is closed? Play with keeping it open and closed throughout the day. What feels better? Does it have messages for you?

Breathe into it and let your Third Eye Chakra talk to you.

What fears are still there from childhood or adulthood that can be let go and forgiven or transmuted when it comes to spirit?

LOOK: Use your imagination and find those denser energies within the chakra and ask why they are there. What are they needing to move through you and let go?

NEW People: I know this may be new to you and seem a little weird or strange in what we are asking you to do—JUST DO IT ☺ This work can be strange and weird and all sorts of adventures can come from it but more importantly all sorts of healing can come from just trying some of the exercises.

Some will work for you and some won't—that is OK.

If you don't "SEE" your Third Eye Chakra, use your imagination—make it up. You will feel your energy shift into a different vibration when you start to get the information your body wants you to hear.

Feel free to post your results and questions in the group.

Notes / Thoughts / Reflections

The *Magic* of Space Clearing

Crown Chakra – 7th Chakra

Location: Right above the top of your head

Color: Violet (I see it as a dark violet but others see it more light) ☺

Emotion: Liberation and spirituality

Gland: Pineal

Organs and Body Parts: Brain, hypothalamus

When Balanced: Universal Energy, cosmic love, enlightenment, spiritual awareness, purpose

Out of Balance: Confinement, closed, mindedness

Health Effects: Depression, insanity, cranial pressure, psychosis

10 ways to activate as well as get in touch with your Crown Chakra

1. Surround yourself with the beautiful violet color.

2. Meditation

3. Close your eyes and look up. Connect with your higher self—breathe it in.

4. Raise your vibration through laughter, dance, breath, fun, and joy!

5. Use your hand to see if you can touch the actual energy of your chakra—you may need a friend to assist.

6. Get a new DO—as in hairdo. Refresh your cut—a new color, new attitude. ☺

7. Music is ALWAYS an easy way to open up and clear all your chakras.

8. Play with stones or crystals. Most crystals open you up and take you higher. Some ground you—pay attention!

9. Engage in the present time. Root Chakra helps to keep us grounded and PRESENT.

10. Connect with the moon. Full moon and new moon—I tend to feel that energy coming in the top of my head each turn of the moon, but you will need to be quiet and centered.

Exercise

I encourage you to close your eyes. Imagine from the top of your head a beautiful white light that sparkles and shines to fill your entire body with white light. Starting from the Crown Chakra all the way down to the tips of your toes. Each chakra getting filled with that beautiful white light.

As you bring your attention to your Crown Chakra I want you to pay attention to what is even higher up than the Crown Chakra—this is the space where you connect with your higher self, your spirit, heaven.

In this space take the time to connect with that higher-self and spirit and ask what it needs from you today. How can you connect that piece of yourself not only with your heart but with your head? We are body, mind and spirit. Create a space that all 3 can work together. Does one part need a break while another part would like to take the lead?

Very often I find the head wants a break and the heart wants to lead.

Before you come back to the room, after this conversation, create a rope of white light from the top of your Crown Chakra all the way to the base of your spine and the Root Chakra. Let that rope go deep down into the earth to be tied tightly around a tree stump to keep you grounded and in your body. When you feel guided simply open your eyes and come back to the room and journal the pieces of conversation that mean the most.

Liberation and Spirituality

The key emotions around the Crown Chakra.

What do you do each day to create liberation and freedom?

What energy needs to move inside of you that would create a space of freedom?

Where do you feel trapped?

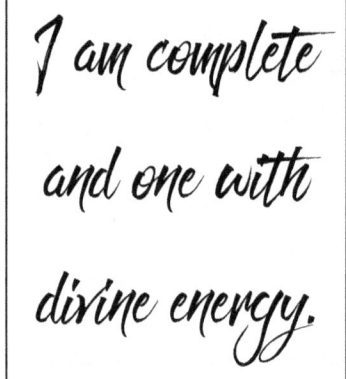

I am complete and one with divine energy.

BREATHE

IDEAS to connect to Crown Chakra

BREATHE: Each day, stop at least five times in a day and breathe into your crown chakra.

Break out of the Box.

Close your eyes.

Imagine the piece of your life that is keeping you from feeling Liberated and FREE.

What does that box look like?

How does it feel?

What does the inside of the box look and feel like?

When you look through the side of the box into the freedom what do you see?

If spirit could give you one tool to break out of that trapped box what would it be?

Let spirit help you.

Receive that one tool that is needed to break you out of that box.

Use it.

Break Free

How does it feel to break it down? Destroy it.

How does freedom feel?

Share on our page this week what you noticed and the aftereffects of breaking free of that box.

You may receive miracles from this one little meditation if you allow it!

Notes / Thoughts / Reflections

_____

_____

_____

_____

_____

5
Checklist for Clearing a Space

Checklist for clearing a space outdoors:

- ✓ Protect your energy—first and foremost!
- ✓ Survey the outside of the home.
- ✓ How does it feel initially—the first moment you drive up?
- ✓ What is the personality of the space?
- ✓ Does it have any messages for you before you start?
- ✓ Have you asked the home for permission to clear it?
- ✓ What do you notice on the outside that could support the house?

- ✓ What does your body feel the space needs the most help with?
- ✓ Ask your dream team for any messages or directions for clearing the outside of the space.

Notes / Thoughts / Reflections

_____
_____
_____
_____
_____
_____
_____
_____
_____
_____
_____
_____
_____
_____
_____
_____
_____
_____
_____
_____
_____
_____
_____

Front Door:

- ✓ What does it say to you?
- ✓ Does the energy feel like its welcoming as you walk in?
- ✓ Does the front door tell a story?
- ✓ Stand in the door to see how the energy feels.
- ✓ The front door is the mouth of the home?
- ✓ Is it getting to express itself?

Notes / Thoughts / Reflections

_____
_____
_____
_____
_____
_____
_____
_____
_____
_____
_____
_____
_____

Family or Client:

- ✓ Why did they call you?
- ✓ What are they hoping to achieve? Is it realistic views of clearing?
- ✓ What are the symptoms the space has shown them?
- ✓ Any issues with health?
- ✓ Sleeping?
- ✓ Children?
- ✓ Animals?
- ✓ Are there spirits in the house?
- ✓ How does the overall inside of the home feel as you survey the space?
- ✓ Does the air seem to move or is it still and stale?
- ✓ Does your body have any reaction to the space?
- ✓ What does your team have to say about the space?
- ✓ Always be gracious with clients—spirit talks with love, you do the same! You can be blunt but loving.
- ✓ If they are in fear, please educate them on vibrations of fear and how to raise that vibration—bring light to the fear.
- ✓ Teach them to call in protection and support, get them involved.
- ✓ Sometimes the talking is the most important part of the clearing.

- ✓ Ask your client which rooms feel the best and the worst to them.
- ✓ Let the client lead followed by your intuition.

Notes / Thoughts / Reflections

Basement or Lowest Floor

- ✓ Overall how does the energy feel?
- ✓ When you walk down the stairs did it feel hard to walk?
- ✓ Is the energy moving or still?
- ✓ Stuck or sticky?
- ✓ Cloudy or grey?
- ✓ Any sense of gremlins?
- ✓ Any sense of spirits?
- ✓ Any sense of fear?
- ✓ Any sense of stuck energy?
- ✓ Any sense of negative vortexes?
- ✓ What dos your team tell you to clear?
- ✓ How do they tell you to clear it?
- ✓ Do you need tools? Sage, holy water, incense, bells, prayer, love?
- ✓ Is the client ready to release that negative energy and if not its ok to work through that in a gentle way?
- ✓ Do the animals have anything to say?
- ✓ What do you SEE with your eyes?

- ✓ What do you sense with your body and intuition?

- ✓ Anything stick out that could be a feng shui? Shift a picture of a sinking ship or anything like that.

- ✓ What energy can you move along?

FILL the space up with what the client would like to create within the family home. If they don't know help them get some clarity.

Notes / Thoughts / Reflections

_____
_____
_____
_____
_____
_____
_____
_____
_____
_____
_____
_____
_____
_____
_____
_____
_____
_____

The *Magic* of Space Clearing

Main Floor

- ✓ What do you notice?
- ✓ How do the corners feel?
- ✓ Do they spend time in this area?
- ✓ Any rooms arguments tend to break out in?
- ✓ What does your team tell you?
- ✓ Anything with the art work or displayed items that need attention?
- ✓ Does the space feel alive?
- ✓ Ask your team what it needs to feel better?
- ✓ What needs to be cleared?
- ✓ Any clutter? That gives a hint to energy that needs to be cleared?
- ✓ How do the windows look? Are they clean?
- ✓ Remember the house resembles the person's body— take notice.
- ✓ Any leaky faucets? That effects the finances.

Water is also a sign of emotional release that is not happening

Upstairs

Use same guidelines as main floor.

Notes / Thoughts / Reflections

Report back to me what you experience as you clear your home. This is part of your homework, so email me this report please!

- ✓ Where did you have some amazing hits?
- ✓ Where did you get stuck?
- ✓ What could you use support with?
- ✓ What could make the clearing easier?
- ✓ Were you in your head or did you stay in your spirit?
- ✓ Any surprises?
- ✓ Any new skills from spirit that you didn't expect?
- ✓ How did your body feel before, during, and after?
- ✓ Did you notice the shifts?
- ✓ Could you feel them or see them or even hear them?

Share your experience!

Notes / Thoughts / Reflections

_____

_____

_____

_____

_____

Conclusion

When we walk into the world of clearing a space, the most important piece is to trust your process.

Clearing is an ever-changing art that has no boundaries. Energy shifts and changes and moves and grows and as you get more comfortable with clearing your space and your energy the skills will grow and you will receive even more insight from spirit on how to do it!

If you are finding value in this work and would like to learn more you can also join me at www.TheSpiritSchool.com

I have worked in the spirit world for nearly 10 years and even though I love everything about it, I always felt something was missing. That something weighed on me heavily almost every minute of every day.

Finally—a bit reluctantly—I started asking spirit to show me the next step and got out of my own way!

Soon, the signs started to show up—the people, the connections, the name and the vision. Believe me, that vision became something bigger than I could have ever imagined.

I always used to talk about having something akin to Hogwarts online, just lighter and more fun. And believe it or not, Hogwarts began sending me magical signs—ridiculously obvious magical signs that told me I was on the right track!

Spirit School has been my heart's desire for years, I just didn't realize it! Long before Spirit School came to be, I told my mentor that all I wanted was a magic wand so I could help people feel better in the world. Little did I know that my magic wand was on its way!

And so the magic continued to come together—the vision, the logo, the course, and then the questions! Such as:

- How do I hear my own angels to tell me my next step?
- Do I have a guardian angel?
- Spiritual stuff scares the shit out of me—how do I move past that?
- I don't think I am intuitive—can I learn how to be?
- How does all this energy stuff work anyway?
- How will it change my life if I talk to spirit? I don't get it.

And then came the big questions, like:

- I think I talk to dead people—isn't that weird?
- I know I have lived before—how do past lives work?
- I feel things and know things and I don't know why—can you help me understand?

And so on.

So, what is Spirit School?

Spirit school is a place to become Spiritually Fearless in your life.

It's a safe space full of like-minded people where you can dig deeper into who you are and what makes you tick.

A place where you can begin to understand the spirit side of yourself—not just that busy head that talks, talks, talks all day long.

A place where you can learn to *feel* your way through life instead of *thinking* your way through.

A place to create magic in your life once you understand how spirit works within YOU.

Spirit School is a Place For You If...

You are open to magic. By magic I mean some pretty strange but cool synchronicities that come as soon as people sign up for my courses!

You like to learn through experience and are self-motivated enough to go out and try things even if they seem uncomfortable or a bit crazy!

You have been feeling that pull that tells you something is waiting for you and you have not figured out what that THING is yet. Yes, we have been waiting for you too!

Spirit is fascinating to you but maybe scares you a little (or a lot). Let me show you a new perspective.

You struggle with managing your own energy in daily life—I bet I know why!

If this feels like the next step for you, please join me at www.TheSpiritSchool.com for the next session of Spirit School starting soon! Let the magic expand!

Bonus Section: Tools

I get a lot of questions about what clearing TOOLS to use when a space or body needs to get clear.

YES, at times when guided I do use tools. Through the years I have gotten a stronger connection with spirit and have felt that I was OK to use tools or **NOT**. So please follow your guidance when any kind of tools are present. Some days you will very much be guided to use them and some days not. **Honor that!**

Let me go over a few of my favorite tools that I use for clearing when guided...

1. SMUDGING

Smudging is a Native American custom designed to clear a space of any negative energy or spirits that may be causing problems in the land of the living. It's a powerful way to clear your home and a fun subject to research if you feel guided.

Supplies:

- Matches
- Smudge stick (you can use sage, cedar, incense)
- A plate to catch ashes
- You might want a feather to steer smoke, but your hand will work just as well!

Start with an intention to clear away any dense or heavy energy and bring light and love into your home. I start in the bottom of my home and work my way up. I just repeat my prayer or affirmation and spend a little extra time in the parts of my home that feel heavy or dark. Then I open windows and doors to allow the energy to move outside where nature can take care of it. I work my way to the top floor and leave through the front door and walk around the house to smudge outside. You can't be too thorough!

2. RING OUT THE BAD JUJU

I learned this from a Feng Shui expert when I had a house full of spirits. We live across from a church and occasionally our home is a bit of a magnet for that energy. When we first moved in I even saw a ghost sitting in one of our rocking chairs.

Supplies:

- One very loud bell

Open everything—drawers, doors, windows, closets, the stove, the fridge, the freezer. Can it be opened? Open it.

Take a very loud bell and starting in the center of your home, ring that bell as loud as you possibly can. Let the sound of the bell resonate through the house.

Starting on the main floor, work your way up and down the house, leaving the doors open so the energy can move outside. Ring the bell in corners, under beds, in closets, anywhere that heavy, dense energy can hide. (Apologize to your pets and neighbors later).

Move. That. Energy. Out. The sound and vibration of the bell moves it back where it belongs.

3. VACCUUM OR SWEEP

When my home needs a quick update or people are stopping by I give my home a quick vacuum. I can immediately feel a shift in my house - it's like a new haircut! This also helps you declutter those spaces that are blocking energy. When you vacuum, the energy moves and you move. All of a sudden you're cleaning and decluttering and your space is clear, clean, and inspiring.

4. GET YOUR BOOGIE ON

Music can change energy within seconds. Seconds! The vibration of your home can be uplifted and changed with the first few bars of a good song! Not surprisingly, moving your body along with the music will bring you your own vibration shift. Bonus points for singing along!

5. SAY A PRAYER

Ask Archangel Michael to enter your home. Here's a prayer that I like from Sunny Dawn Johnston:

"I invoke the blue light of Archangel Michael to surround and protect this home from any negative energy or entities, seen or unseen ... and so it is!"

Don't be afraid to feel your way through this and do it in a way that works for you—open or closed eyes, saying a prayer to whomever or whatever works for you.

6. HAVE YOUR HOUSE CLEARED

Ideas 1-5 are totally doable, totally implementable, powerful ways to clear away the surface energy that affects us. So maybe you're feeling just a little bit stuck. A tiny bit uninspired. Not 100% totally-over-the-top in love with your life.

And you're not sure why, exactly, you feel like this.

But you know that as soon as you walk through your front door you feel tired and overwhelmed and, honestly, kinda crappy. All of a sudden, you just want to nap or watch terrible TV or pick a fight about the nearly empty milk carton.

Yuck.

But **clearing** goes deeper. We head into the foundation that needs healing and dig into the deeper part of your home that needs help. When we go deep into your home, we're going deep into your own fears + blocks and freeing your home and your heart.

Clearing moves energy in huge ways; doors to opportunity are opened + life begins to heal + move forward.

Goodbye, stuck!

Adios, stale, uninspired space!

About The Author

Jodie Harvala is a forward thinking, spirit loving, space clearing, psychic teacher and coach. She is also the founder of The Spirit School. Walking through her own spirit journey she went from a fear *based* woman to a spiritually fearless entrepreneur

Jodie loves teaching others how to connect with spirit and also how to experience spirit in the sacred, every day moments of life. She teaches through experience with each and every class offered, people who participate walk away with their own very real experience with spirit and a fresh perspective regarding the next step on their personal journal here on earth.

Jodie shares tools and ideas to connect with spirit on a daily basis, creating your own magical experience day to day. When you walk through life with direction from spirit, we become fearless. With each course offered from Spirit School you will feel empowered and filled with magic in your own life. Hands on your hearts ladies and gentleman Its time to pledge allegiance to your higher self. All aboard the bus to Spirit School!

Other Books and Products by Jodie Harvala:

BOOKS:
ABC's of Intuition: A 26-Day Guide to Spirit
Living Your Purpose with Sunny Dawn Johnston & Friends

CARD DECKS:
Living Your Purpose Affirmation Cards
The Wonderment Oracle Deck

MP3/CD's:
The 5 Clairs
Time to be Brave
Transforming Anxiety
Meditation Bundle

www.JodieHarvala.com

The Magic of Space Clearing

www.ingramcontent.com/pod-product-compliance
Lightning Source LLC
Chambersburg PA
CBHW071726090426
42738CB00009B/1891